CANYON IN THE BODY

CANYON IN THE BODY
身体里的峡谷

Selected Poetry of

Lan Lan
蓝蓝

Translated from Chinese by Fiona Sze-Lorrain

Zephyr Press & The Chinese University Press of Hong Kong
Brookline, Mass | Hong Kong

Cover image by Xu Bing
Book design by *typeslowly*
Printed in Hong Kong

Several of the poems and translations first appeared in
*Antigonish Review, Brooklyn Rail (InTranslation), Cerise Press,
Crazyhorse, Hayden's Ferry Review, Mānoa, Pathlight, Poetry East West,
Poetry London, Poetry Review, Salamander, Stand Magazine, Upstairs at Duroc,* and *Vallum.*

Five translations were published in a hand-bound chapbook *You Are Not Here*
(The Offending Adam, 2012) in a limited bilingual edition of 300 copies.

A pocket bilingual edition of twenty poems, *Nails*, was also published
by The Chinese University Press on the occasion of the 2013
International Poetry Nights in Hong Kong.

This publication is supported by the Jintian Literary Foundation.
Zephyr Press also acknowledges with gratitude the financial support
of the Massachusetts Cultural Council.

massculturalcouncil.org

Zephyr Press, a non-profit arts and education 501(c)(3) organization,
publishes literary titles that foster a deeper understanding of cultures
and languages. Zephyr Press books are distributed to the trade in the U.S.
and Canada by Consortium Book Sales and Distribution [www.cbsd.com]
and by Small Press Distribution [www.spdbooks.org].

Published for the rest of the world by:
The Chinese University Press
The Chinese University of Hong Kong
Sha Tin, N.T., Hong Kong

Cataloguing-in publication data is available from the Library of Congress.

ZEPHYR PRESS
www.zephyrpress.org

JINTIAN
www.jintian.net

THE CHINESE UNIVERSITY PRESS
www.chineseupress.com

CONTENTS

短句 Short Lines

I   INDEED

II   A WEIGHT   AND A BALANCE

V   PASSWORD IN THIS NIGHT

I Speak to Rivers and Silence —
Lyricism in Lan Lan's Poetry

Lyrical poetry is a confident art that moves outward and into difficult realms. It contains a fleeting glimpse of the familiar order in a studied arrangement that defines its stylistic life. But surely, even apologists for this art, "hearers and hearteners of the work,"[1] know how impossible it must be to commit to this practice without the urgency of social preoccupations and intellectual drive: will lyrical poetry stand in danger of being perceived as "pleasing words or sounds," devoid of an immediate rhetoric, a sustained sense of narrative gravity and architecture?

Considered one of today's most influential Chinese lyrical writers, Lan Lan emerged as a representative woman poet during the early nineties. A consistent presence in the mainland literary scene, her writing renews the need to address lyricism when the dominant cultural discourse favors phallocentrism and the privilege of human over non-human. Born in 1967 to a soldier father and a peasant mother in Yantai, a village in Shandong province, Lan Lan grew up with her grandmother in rural Henan and Shandong. Away from the blows of the Cultural Revolution, she saw the carefree joys of childhood. From a young age, nature spoke to her: charmed by its mysteries, silence and changes, she learned to live in intimate harmony with the pastoral world. Lan Lan's grandmother was a talented storyteller. She engaged the child's imagination with magical fables and folk tales, encouraging her to indulge in books and play. Origins for much of the poet's adult work are meditative impressions of the disquieting and the enigmatic in a rural world where trees run and rivers gossip. Of these early days of bliss and innocence, the poet recalls with nostalgia and in present tense: "I go to a school where my classroom is a cowshed and our

---

1. Yeats, W. B. "At Galway Races." *The Collected Poems of W. B. Yeats.* New York: Simon & Schuster, 1996. 97.

'desks' made of sun-dried mud brick. Right behind us are a large pile of peanut vines and two yellow cattle."[2]

At fourteen, Lan Lan published her first sequence of poems, "I Want to Sing," in a renowned literary journal based in Wuhan, *Fragrant Grass*. Her impassioned desire to "sing," *cantabile* — the verb that defines her literary debut — enacts the Greek ideal that great poetry must be celebrated as music. "Sing, goddess," proclaims Homer in his invocation to the Muse at the start of *The Iliad*. Another Chinese poet Hai Zi[3] also extolled the commitment to songs as an ideal for lyric poetry: "To become a poet you must . . . endure what must be endured, sing what must be sung."[4] Apart from the singer as a recurring persona — take for instance, the eponymous poem "Singer" — the vocal emphasis in Lan Lan's poetic behavior is part of the narrator's image and pathos. "A line of words. Transmitting your voice / into my body in soundless waves," she discloses in "Secret Lover." Heard through a line of words, the voice now imposes itself as an erotic agent that physicalizes the sonic allure through earthly sensations and non-discursive effects.

Hoping to pursue her passion in the literary world, Lan Lan experienced a series of setbacks at the start. Fragile in health, she moved with her family from village to village and bore the heavy loss of her grandmother, who died in the year when the end of the Cultural Revolution coincided with the Tangshan earthquake. She fainted during her high school examination and had to abandon the prospect of college studies for a working life — as a factory worker packaging wine, a crane operator, and a technical writer.

---

2. My translation; see the poet's biographical chronology in *Selected Poems of Lan Lan*. Beijing: Poetry and People, 2009. 115.

3. Considered a major Chinese poetic voice, Hai Zi (1964–1989) has a posthumous cult-like status in China. Born and raised in a farming village in Anhui province, he passed the entrance exam to the prestigious Beijing University at fifteen. At twenty, he started teaching philosophy and art theory at China University of Political Science and Law. During his brief yet explosive life, he wrote about 250 poems and several epics, portraying an intense mix of illuminating and complex visions of his difficult society. Hai Zi committed suicide in 1989 by laying himself on a railroad track at Beijing Shanhaiguan. He was twenty-five.

4. Hai Zi. "Excerpt from 'The Poet I Most Love — Hölderlin.'" Trans. Gerald Maa. *Chinese Writers on Writing*. Ed. Arthur Sze. San Antonio: Trinity University Press, 2010. 184.

These rugged years of labor, living at the bottom of society, instilled in Lan Lan empathy and broadened her understanding of life in a way that was both tangible and real. During this time, she grew close to the working class; cobblers, blacksmiths, and carpenters would later come to life in her oeuvre. She also read voraciously and became self-taught in poetry, philosophy, and history. In the concluding poem of this book, "A Poet's Work," Lan Lan epitomizes the poet as a blacksmith in an analogous way that the Irish poet Seamus Heaney trades "spade-work for pen work"[5] in "Digging."[6] In meanings more symbolic than situational, it marks the poet's own acknowledgment of these early working years as a foreshadowing course to her writing life.

In 1985, with her hard-earned wages and savings, Lan Lan self-printed her first chapbook, *Red Handkerchief,* the title resonant of a striking image in Czeslaw Milosz's "Happiness": "Farther, under the arch of ancient ruins / You see a few tiny walking figures. / One wears a red kerchief. There are trees, / Ramparts and mountains at an early hour."[7] The following year, Lan Lan was admitted into a college in Zhengzhou. With a degree in journalism, she later found work at a provincial literary union before being hired as a poetry editor and art director at a local mainstream literary journal, *Big River.*

Upon the publication of her first "official" collection, *Life with a Smile* (1990), the poet came to national attention with an epiphanic work of odes to nature and its unsayable mysteries. With these early poems, she succeeded in establishing herself as a naturalistic writer. Marveling at the way she unfurled consciousness and receptivity through wonder, fulfilment, and gratitude in her poetry, critics described her writing as the space of "strong

5. Heaney, Seamus. "'The hazel stirred': *Death of a Naturalist.*" Interview by Dennis O'Driscoll. *Stepping Stones: Interviews with Seamus Heaney.* London: Faber and Faber, 2008. 66.

6. "Under my window, a clean rasping sound / When the spade sinks into gravelly ground: / My father, digging ... Between my finger and my thumb / The squat pen rests. / I'll dig with it." Heaney, Seamus. "Digging." *Death of a Naturalist.* London: Faber and Faber, 1966. 13–14.

7. Milosz, Czeslaw. "Happiness." Trans. Richard Lourie. *Selected Poems.* New York: Ecco Press, 1973. 19.

musicality and rhythmic silence." Encouraged by a positive reception and her growing readership, Lan Lan widened her writing scope; she tried her hand at lyrical prose and started publishing children's fiction.

Since the nineties, Lan Lan has authored over a dozen books of poetry and lyrical prose, which include the bestselling titles, *Songs of Romance* (1993), *Inner Life* (1997), *Night Has a Face* (2001), *Sleep, Sleep* (2003), and *From Here, to Here* (2010). A single mother with twin teenage daughters under her care, she taught for a few years before devoting herself to full-time writing. She resides in Beijing but returns to her hometown village for retreats. In Henan she finds the opportunity to dedicate language to places. The villages of Xuying and Xiaodian, Ruins of the Great River Village . . . these are sites from her native province where collective history contends with personal stories. Train journeys and nights have, too, become an inexhaustible source of inspiration for poetry. When we last met in Paris in the spring of 2012, she was working on a cartoon script and a book of fairy tales. An active advocate for child welfare — the poet campaigns for education reforms — she still keeps up with the discipline of one poem each week.

The range of Lan Lan's reading interests is broad yet selective. She cites Dostoyevsky, Kafka, and Blake, and studies Chinese classical poetry — the *Nineteen Ancient Poems of the Han Dynasty*, the *Book of Odes,* and the Tang poems — as well as translations of Francis Jammes, René Char, Wallace Stevens, and Juan Ramón Jiménez. An eclectic reader of history, philosophy, folklore, astronomy, botany, and geography, she refers to sociobiological studies, plant catalogues, and ancient texts of Chinese herbology. In an essay on nature in her poetry, Lan Lan names the Russian author Boris Sergunenkov (1931–) as an influence, an unfashionable choice to say the least, for little of his work is known outside or within Russia.

When I started on this translation, I came across a review article that described her poems as maintaining "warm temperatures and sensibilities." The analogy "warm temperatures" is a refreshing take on a work that explores romance and womanhood with unabashed femininity, while depicting a receding natural world through an urban lens. In stark simplicity and sparseness of words, time becomes so small and slow that it is strangely immortal and erotic. To revisit Milosz: "Rivers grow small. Cities grow small. And splendid gardens / show what we did not see there before: crippled leaves and dust."[8] As a woman, I am naturally sensitive to Lan Lan's discreet though courageous endorsement of her identity as a woman, wife, mother, sister, girlfriend, and lover as a point of departure in her work, a stance that remains marginalized in the largely patriarchal Chinese society. Measures to redeem sexist dogmas are subtle but quick. While tenderness does not come free, her sincerity is what endears the reader to the words, as is the case for her desire to refrain from loud feminist polemics:

> Your hand tells me what I'm becoming:
>   woman.
> Neither a flower
> nor an anonymous poem
> — is this also real?

> — "Startle"

Presented in five thematic sections, this bilingual collection compiles Lan Lan's most characteristic work as it showcases her lyricism, austerity, luminosity, and moral sensibilities. Many of these poems have been anthologized in China and abroad. However, other than two translations in *Push Open the Window* (Copper Canyon Press, 2010) and a sampling in *Another Kind of Nation: An Anthology of Contemporary Chinese Poetry* (Talisman House, 2007), none of her poetry exists in English in a coherent entirety. The poet and I surveyed the choice and matrix of poems that could allow forays into her aesthetic tension and conceptual engagement with image, silence, and words. In the opening poem, for instance, specific choices in punctuation and lineation result in a visual and aural construct

---

8. *Ibid.*, "Rivers Grow Small." 28.

of the poem as both experience and gesture:

> I like this —
> madness. The stillest.
>
> You drag in experience to love me, yet fear
> using it to know me.

— "Short Lines"

However abstruse it may seem, each line is the flesh of a thought or intuition, illustrating how shapeliness and punctuation — the gradient of diction, the organic form of words and non-words — play an anchoring role in Lan Lan's poetic structure. There is an aesthetic pose to the poem that does not compromise its complex psychological underpinnings or voice-driven pacing. While the atmosphere becomes a formal concern, punctuation is an actor that makes silence more accurate. Compared to most contemporary Chinese poets, Lan Lan exercises more liberty — and innovation — with punctuation: more dashes and ellipses exist in her work, with periods disposed to interpretation, not judgment. For these reasons, my translation hopes to retain the shape of its source version: I find in the shapeliness an integrity that speaks about the poem's inner life, its scent, its (dis)order and balance, its pregnability and boundaries, as well as the information it hopes to convey. Visually, it renders to the poem a dramatic and ravishing visibility — a body, a *mode of becoming*, a *presence*.

In the poems of eros, prayer, and meditation, each carries a quiet address, a letter waiting to be read. In several of them, the addressee remains a mystery. Mystery fuels desire. Often, there exists a veil between the speaker and the listener. In poems that speak of love and longing, pronouns such as "you" and "I" are either transparent or interchangeable, both singular and implicitly plural. At once conspiratorial and capricious, the "I" is capable of resisting and luring the "you" before inhabiting the second-person pronoun. Ownership and identity become so porous that individual moments and emotions are more empowered than plots. No need for biographical spin, the transitory narratives in Lan Lan's poetry seem unconventional, that is, more inwardly thwarted and free of linear progression. They are governed by a gaze that alters from stanza to stanza, or more radically, from word to word. This turned gaze behaves independently of its voice, which in turn generates other possibilities of ventriloquism. Consider "You Are," in which a deceptively simple invocation of autumn contains multiple voices and echoes before the duplicity of selves and reflections reveals itself:

> autumn. You say.
> (Are you autumn?)
>
> Listen, the shuffling of poplars.
> (Are you the shuffling of poplars?)
>
> Sit on the grass.
> (Are you grass, or is grass you?)
>
> And bauhinias —
> now I see you,
>
> and those you bring along
> but you are not them
> they are not you

> — "You Are"

If language must be used to do the work of image, Lan Lan believes it is important to distinguish the visible from the real, and the real from reality. The juxtaposition of vision and feeling is a central theme in her poetry. "Sight is touch," she begins intuitively in "The Blind," a poem that suggests a fear of self-revelation and confession. The protagonist represents alignments of identity and self-discovery that voice a struggle between metaphysical acceptance and rhetorical denial. In fact, the poet states — without conscious Buddhist connotation — that "sight as touch" is the *middle way* to truth within the larger practice of lyricism. Touch, the sensory grip closest to the flesh, connects us physically to what is beyond ourselves. This is her *way*, a gradual means of discovery. Mistrusting the seen or unseen, she casts doubts on "absolute" values and details that cloud one's vision.

In recent years — as seen from her latest volume, *From Here, to Here* (2010) — the poet steadily explores socio-political concerns in the aftermath of natural disasters, without jeopardizing her signature sensuality, in dramatic monologues and poems of testimony such as "Vérité," "Train, Train," "A Few Grains of Sand," "Poets Are Useless," "Now, Untouchable," and "Unfinished Voyage." Mindful of how political poems easily become media products instead of a spiritual resistance in fast-modernizing China, she delves deeper into the corporeal experience of word play and image. On the surface, these thematic shifts produce landscapes and contexts that are less mediated, but the experience of *what is said* and *what is told* remains largely subjective. As a critical reader from another culture, I am aware of the linguistic polish, the political accuracy that exists by tints and degrees in some poems. I should also mention "sentimentality," a general criticism of such writing. Invisible love is a strong undercurrent in many of these poems, or at least, in the tone of them. Love poems, particularly those from the final section "Password in This Night," leave the reader with a torn experience of love and absence that Sappho has described as *glukupikron* — "bittersweet," an emotional paradox.[9] But the triumph isn't this sensory intelligence; it is the unconditional shelter Lan Lan wants or creates for her readers. In "Chestnut Tree in the Wind," she states: "To meet you while alive / is enough for me." I observe how feelings — joys, grief, anger, passion, kindness, and forgiveness — are distilled gradually through a contemporary lexicon. On elegaic subjects, the poet censors

---

9. See Carson, Anne. "Bittersweet." *Eros the Bittersweet*. Champaign and London: Dalkey Archive Press, 1998. 3–9.

morbidity. Nothing is cluttered in her private letters. No hysterical voice, no declarative sentence. Instead, we find memories — stories behind a story — that expand through small moments, and it is the music that provides the conduit. A silent space is physically embedded between word groupings, which lends the writing a quality of timelessness.

Of their restraint, the poems carry the secret of all art — distance. Translation lays bare what is approximated. The challenge has to do with the color choice of words. I have approached each poem as an impressionist painting. Before mapping it in English, I close my eyes and recall what I have read and seen in its source language, trying to memorize my first contact with each linguistic detail. How best to maintain the tone, the feel, the "plasticity" and emotional character of words strikes me as the key to this project. For rhyme and breath to operate with little tension and pull, I seek the bass note and the glissando in their sonority and phonetic effect. Ultimately, when one thing falls short in translation, another surrendering instant will occur. *When wind ends, water begins*, muses Lan Lan.[10] Between such moments, I take a deep breath, wait for a point of stillness and concentration to emerge within the work, then sit back to re-enter it, from lip to ear. This time, not word by word — but silence by silence.

Fiona Sze-Lorrain
Paris, France — May 2012

---

10. My translation; see Lan Lan. "Water and Wind." *False Oat-grass (Yanmaicao)*. Beijing: Overseas Chinese Press, 2008. 119.

CANYON IN THE BODY

短句

已经晚了。在我
迷路之前。

我喜欢这个——
疯狂。这最安静的。

可以拖着你所经历的来爱我但恐惧于
　　用它认识我。

我将是你获得世界的一种方式：
每样事物都不同因而是
　　同一种。

Short Lines

Already late. Before I
get lost.

I like this —
madness. The stillest.

You drag in experience to love me, yet fear
        using it to know me.

I'll be a way you reach for the world:
everything is different, so it's
        the same.

I INDEED

真实

死人知道我们的谎言。在清晨
林间的鸟知道风。

果实知道大地之血的灌溉
哭声知道高脚杯的体面。

喉咙间的石头意味着亡灵在场
喝下它！猛兽的车轮需要它的润滑——

碾碎人，以及牙齿企图说出的真实。
世界在盲人脑袋的裂口里扭动

……黑暗从那里来

Vérité

The dead know our lies. At dawn
forest birds know the wind.

Fruits know irrigation from the land's blood
Cries know the dignity of a wine glass.

Stones in my throat signify dead souls
Drink it! Wheels of beasts' carts need grease —

crushing man, and the truth that teeth try to speak.
The world twists in the cracks of a blind skull

. . . where the dark arrives

请和我谈谈幸福

请和我谈谈幸福。请坐在树下
透过枸桃黑黝黝的枝叶
星星在颤抖
孩子们的喧闹声低了
蛐蛐儿的弦歌更亮

请和我谈谈幸福。灶火旁
农妇的脸闪着柴草彤红的光芒
一绺灰发温顺地垂下
羊倌老汉的嘴在酒盅上
　　　呧砸作响

请和我谈谈幸福，在天穹下
牲口们嚼着夜间的草料
你习惯于微笑的嘴角
——它们藏起了多少事情
——默不作声

Please Discuss Happiness with Me

Please discuss happiness with me. Please sit under the tree
Stars quiver
through dark paper mulberry leaves
Children lower their noise
Crickets heighten their *pizzicato*

Please discuss happiness with me. By the stove fire
a peasant woman's face beams in the firewood's radiance
A lock of gray hair droops softly
An old shepherd smacks his lips loudly
       on a wine cup

Please discuss happiness with me, under the sky
beasts of burden graze at night forage
your mouth with corners fond of smiles
— they hide many things
— not a word

永远里有……

永远里有几场雨。一阵阵微风；
永远里有无助的悲苦，黄昏落日时
　　茫然的愣神；

有苹果花在死者的墓地纷纷飘落；
有歌声，有万家灯火的凄凉；

有两株麦穗，一朵云

将它们放进你的蔚蓝。

Inside Eternity . . .

A few bands of rain inside eternity. Breezes;
forlorn inside eternity, the sunset at dusk
      a blank gaze;

apple blossoms fall in a graveyard;
singing, desolate myriad city lights;

two ears of wheat, a cloud

put them into your sky-blue.

蓝色药片

你有个秘密。你有说不出的耻辱。
这圆圆的东西里压缩着
你半生的噩梦。

它统治睡眠，把守夜晚的关隘
在你和死亡开战的床头。

所谓尊严只值几个分币——来吧
和它签订合约，当晨光
脆弱的防线在黑暗前溃败。

它是最后一道战壕，你知道
这无可治愈的病，犹如狂风窜上城垛
撕碎你的旗。

蓝色药片
消减你经历的疼痛。它的爪子
从颅骨里掏出你一团团神经
把泥浆灌进脑袋，为了

使它成为一块石头。

Blue Pill

You have a secret. You have an inexpressible shame.
Half a lifetime of nightmares compressed
into this round object.

It governs sleep, a mountain pass guards the night
at your bedside where you battle against death.

This so-called dignity is only worth a few cents — come,
sign a contract with it, when morning light's
weak defensive lines are crushed before the dark.

It's the last trench, you know
this incurable illness, like a violent wind fleeing up the rampart
ripping your flag.

The blue pill
relieves your pain. Its claw
pulls out wads of nerves from your skull
pouring mud into the brain, to

render it into a stone.

诗人无用

无用的字，无用的眼泪
无用的瘟疫在壮大它的无用
无用凌辱被它毁掉的
    单数的人

水是泪滴，米饭是沙粒
馒头是坚硬的石块
卧室是深渊，厨房是黑暗
每一次呼吸都是被死亡追赶的哀号

无用于最漂亮的面具
无用于一张被劣质水泥板砸碎的
女人的脸，雨水中白皙大腿的腐烂

一场地震加深了地狱的血盆大口
无用的痛哭冲刷迷惘的眼
谁能看见活着的可耻习惯？

没救的人，依然在喝死人的血
犹如这几行文字
在加深我的耻辱、窒息——
写下它：
罪责仍在继续……

Poets Are Useless

Useless words, useless tears
Useless plague expanding its uselessness
Uselessness insults each and every one
           it has destroyed

Water is a teardrop, rice a grain of sand
A steamed bun is solid stone
Bedroom an abyss, a kitchen the darkness
Each breath an anguished howl chased by death

Useless to the loveliest mask
Useless to a woman's face smashed by weak
cement slabs, a fair thigh decaying in the rain

An earthquake deepens the bloody maw of hell
Useless wails cleanse perplexed eyes
Who can see the shameful routine of an ignoble life?

Hopeless men, still drinking blood from the dead
Like these lines
deepening my disgrace, my suffocation —
write it down:
Guilt still goes on . . .

读史

庞大的帝国建立起来了。八方臣服的
小国聚集一起，繁荣和交流
上百年的和平就要在盛宴后
开始。

异域的瓜果，交易和通婚
多么好，一个伟大国家的诞生！

而你在另一本考古典籍中读到
出土的残片记载了一个士兵
如何在那场战争里失去了妻子、女儿
和一条左腿。

你看不到残片。但你也扔掉了那本
正确和合法的史书。

Studying History

A vast empire is built. With universal allegiance
small nations gather, in prosperity, with exchanges
A century of peace will begin after
the banquet.

Foreign fruits, trade and intermarriage
How wonderful, the birth of a great nation!

Yet in another ancient book of archaeology you read
how a soldier from the excavated ruins
lost his wife, daughter, and left leg
in the war.

You can't see the ruins. But you've also thrown away that
factual and authorized book of historical records.

鞋匠之死

那时他放下粪桶，在徐营村头
傍晚。一个鞋匠为兄弟
干着他的手艺活
木楦子变得沉闷
黑色泥泞，从脚趾缝里向悲哀打开
熟悉的贫困朝笔尖讨债。
雨越下越大。破窗棂上的纸
瑟瑟作响，风劈开他和省城会议桌上的缝隙。

在寒冷中变绿，萝卜地的田埂
印上了趔趄的脚印。
再也没有牛被他买去，拴在课桌腿上。
他只想笑，也这么

做了。墨水瓶底还有一层结冰的洋油
灯芯静静地烧。补丁盖不住暴力的
裂口。锤头。他缝着雨和黑暗，为了

无人继承的遗产：砧子上
一根钉子将痛苦深深地
砸进他的脑袋。

只有被遗弃的鞋知道——徐玉诺，
河南诗人，死于1958年。
赤脚，带着疯子的绰号和将来之花园
向丘陵和平原逶迤而去，身后
是跟随他的群山。

Death of a Cobbler

At the entrance of Xuying Village, he put down the shit buckets
Evening. A cobbler practiced
his craft for his brother
The wooden last turned gloomy
Black mud, opening into sorrow from between the toes
A familiar poverty demanded repayment from the pen tip.
Rain poured more and more. Tattered lattice windows with rattling
paper, wind split open a crack between him and the provincial city's
                                                    conference table.

Turning green in the cold, ridges in carrot fields
bore prints of staggering footsteps.
No more cows for him to buy, to be tied to a school table leg.
He just wanted to laugh, and so he

did. And a coat of kerosene frozen at the bottom of the inkpot
A wick quietly burned. The mend could not make up for the fissure
of violence. Hammerhead. He stitched rain and darkness, for

a legacy no one would inherit: on the anvil
a nail drove misery deep
into his head.

Only abandoned shoes would know — Xu Yunuo,
poet from Henan, died 1958.
Barefoot, nicknamed *madman*, he took *Garden of the Future*
into hills and plains, meandering with
mountains behind him.

我的笔

蘸满肮脏的泥水，我的笔
有着直立的影子。一棵陡峭的树
从那里生长。我的笔

钻进垃圾箱翻捡
弯下的身躯在纸上爬行。我的笔
要钉住大皮靴燃烧的脚印
挖掘被活埋的东西。

它准备放弃天赋、流水账
插进坚硬的石头。石头。
它记录噩梦，记录弯曲的影子
真诚是它的哨兵。我的笔

折回它的翅膀，向下钻
直到岩层下的哀嚎握住它——
火和油。这是我想要的。

每一声被称之为诗的哭泣都想要的。

My Pen

Dipped in muddy water, my pen
casts a vertical shadow. A steep tree grows
from there. My pen

digs into a trash bin and rummages
its bent body crawling across paper. My pen
wants to nail down burning footprints by leather boots
digging out things that were buried alive.

It is ready to give up talent, daily accounts
stuck in solid stone. Stone.
It records nightmares, records curving shadows
Sincerity is its sentry. My pen

folds back its wings, dips downward
until wails beneath rock layers hold it tight —
fire and oil. This is what I want.

What each fit of weeping known as poetry would want.

震惊

仇恨是酸的，腐蚀自己的独腿
恶是地狱，装着恶的身躯。

眼珠在黑白中转动
犹如人在善恶里运行：

——我用它看见枝头的白霜
美在低处慢慢结冰

居然。

Shock

Hatred is sour, corroding its one leg
Evil is hell, packed with evil bodies.

An eyeball rotates in black and white
like man shifting between good and evil:

— I use this notion to see frost on branch tips
Beauty is slowly freezing beneath

Indeed.

失眠

我睡不着。

我的皮肤下有一场政变。
四周的一切已是另一个朝代。
我可以确信，阳台上的花朵
开始飞去
孤寂渗出砖缝，与世界
　　　汇合。

我睡不着。

整座城市被移走
一列列街树奔跑起来。
我确信某个粒子改变了速度。
虽然，我坐在桌前
而墙壁——一动不动。

Insomnia

I can't sleep.

A *coup d'état* under my skin.
A new dynasty all around.
I can be sure, flowers on the balcony
are flying away
Solitude seeps from a mortar joint, merging
        with the world.

I can't sleep.

The whole city is removed
Trees along the streets start to run row by row.
I'm certain a particle has changed its speed.
Though I'm sitting at the table
walls — static.

更多的是沉默

更多的是沉默。
雁群中秘密的磁针。

有多少笑容浮现在人群中
仿佛枝叶的喧响
……阳光　　栖鸟
生活的欢乐。

沉默是不道德的。
沉默中有一只最大的耳朵。

沉默只能听见沉默那深夜里
　　沉重的喘息——

What Is More Is Silence

What is more is silence.
A secret magnetic needle among wild geese.

Many smiles emerge from the crowd
like boisterous branches and leaves
. . . sunlight   dwelling birds
the joys of life.

Silence isn't ethical.
Silence has the largest ear.

Silence can only hear silence's heavy panting
              late at night —

火车，火车

黄昏把白昼运走。窗口从首都
摇落到华北的沉沉暮色中

……从这里，到这里。

道路击穿大地的白杨林
闪电，会跟随着雷
但我们的嘴已装上安全的消声器。

火车越过田野，这页删掉粗重脚印的纸。
我们晃动。我们也不再用言词
帮助低头的羊群，砖窑的滚滚浓烟。

轮子慢慢滑进黑夜。从这里
到这里。头顶不灭的星星
一直跟随，这场墓地漫长的送行
在我们勇气的狭窄铁轨上延伸

火车。火车。离开报纸的新闻版
驶进乡村木然的冷噤：
一个倒悬在夜空中
垂死之人的看。

Train, Train

Dusk carts day away. From the capital the window
swings down into the deep twilight of North China

. . . from here, to here.

A road pierces through the aspen forest
Lightning, then thunder
yet silencers have safely covered our mouths.

The train crosses the field, a page erasing clumsy footsteps.
We sway. We no longer use words
to help goats with bowed heads, smoke billowing from brick kilns.

Wheels slide slowly into night. From here
to here. Overhead, ardent stars
trail behind, this long farewell in a graveyard
stretches along the thin railway of our courage

Train. Train. Pulling out from a newshole in a journal
driving into the numb shivers of villages:
a look from the dying
hanging upside-down in the night sky.

未完成的途中

……午夜。一行字呼啸着
冲出黑暗的隧道。幽蓝的信号灯
闪过。一列拖着脐带的火车
穿越桥梁，枕木下
我凹陷的前胸不断震颤。它紧抵
俯身降落的天空，碾平，伸展
——你知道，我

总是这样，摇晃着
在深夜起身，喝口水
坐下。信。电话线中嗡嗡的雪原。躺在
键盘上被自己的双手运走。翻山越岭
从水杉的尖顶上沉沉扫过，枝条
划破饥渴的脸。或者，贴着地面
冰碴挂上眉毛，你知道，有时

我走在纬四路的楝树下，提着青菜
推门，仿佛看到你的背影，孩子们快乐尖叫
冲过来抱着我的腿。雨从玻璃上滴落。
屋子晃动起来，轮子无声地滑行
拖着傍晚的炊烟。那时，市声压低了

楼下的钉鞋匠，取出含在嘴里的钉子
抡起铁锤，狠狠地楔进生活的鞋底，毫不
犹豫。这些拾荒的人
拉着破烂的架子车，藏起捡到的分币
粗大的骨节从未被摧毁。你知道，端午时节

Unfinished Voyage

. . . Midnight. A line of words howls
dashing out of a dark tunnel. A blue signal lamp
flashes. A train drags its umbilical cord
across the bridge, beneath sleepers
my hollow chest can't stop shaking. It resists
the bow of a fallen sky, flattens, and expands
— you know, I

am always this way, wavering
to get up late at night, take a sip of water
and sit down. Mail. Snowfields hum in the phone. Lying on
the keyboard, carried away by my own hands. Over mountains and valleys
sweeping heavily past the tips of dawn redwoods, branches
slash my starved and craving face. Or close to the ground
ice crystals over my eyebrows, you know, sometimes

I walk under white cedars along Weisi Road, carrying vegetables
pushing open the door, as if I could see your back silhouette, children
                                    shriek with joy
rushing to hug my legs. Rain drips from the windowpane.
The house shakes, wheels glide past without a sound
hauling the kitchen smoke in the evening. City noise subsides

Downstairs, a cobbler plucks a nail from his mouth
lifts a hammer, drives it violently into life's sole, without
hesitation. These rag-and-bone men
pull broken carts, hide any coins they find
their thick joints never worn out. You know, at the Dragon Boat Festival

蒿草浓烈的香气中，我们停靠的地方
布谷鸟从深夜一直叫到天亮，在远处的林子里
躲在树荫下面。你睫毛长长的眼睛
闭着。手边是放凉的水杯和灰烬的余烟。站在窗前，
我想：我爱这个世界。在那
裂开的缝隙里，我有过机会。
它缓缓驶来，拐了弯……

我总是这样。盯着荧屏，长久地
一行字跳出黑暗。黝黝的田野。矿灯飞快地向后
丘陵。水塘。夜晚从我的四肢碾过。
凄凉。单调。永不绝望
你知道，此时我低垂的额头亮起
一颗星：端着米钵。摇动铁轮的手臂
被活塞催起——火苗窜上来。一扇窗口
飘着晾晒的婴儿尿布，慢慢升高了……

in thick wormwood aroma, we stop where
cuckoos call from late night till daybreak, lying under the shade of trees
in distant woods. Your long lashed eyes
are closed. At hand, a cup of water turning cold and the last smoke from
ashes. Before the window,
I think *I love this world*. There
a fissure opens, my chance is here.
Slowly it steers toward me, around the curve . . .

I am always this way. Staring forever at the screen
A line of words jumps out of the dark. Black fields. A miner's lamp
flies backward
Hills. Ponds. Night runs over my limbs.
Desolation. Monotony. Never despair
You know, at this moment, on my bowed forehead glows
a star: I carry a rice bowl. Arms moving iron wheels
are driven by a piston — flames gush up. From a window
drying diapers flutter, and slowly rise . . .

II A WEIGHT AND A BALANCE

一切的理由

我的唇最终要从人的关系那早年的
　　蜂巢深处被喂到一滴蜜。

不会是从花朵。
也不会是星空。

假如它们不像我的亲人
它们也不会像我。

Reason for Everything

Finally my lips are fed by a honeydrop deep in a honeycomb
                lineage from an earlier time.

Not from flowers.
Nor the starry sky.

If they weren't like my kin
they aren't like me.

你是

秋天。你说。
（你是秋天？）

听，杨树的沙沙声。
（你是杨树的沙沙声？）

坐在草地上。
（你是草地，或者草地是你？）

还有羊蹄甲花——
现在我看见你了，

和你带来的它们
但你不是它们
它们不是你

杨树的沙沙声不是。
草地不是。还有
羊蹄甲花也不是。

You Are

autumn. You say.
(Are you autumn?)

Listen, the shuffling of poplars.
(Are you the shuffling of poplars?)

Sit on the grass.
(Are you grass, or is grass you?)

And bauhinias —
now I see you,

and those you bring along
but you are not them
they are not you

Not the shuffling of poplars.
Not grass. And
not bauhinias.

拥有很少东西的人

蠡斯和蟋蟀
绿衣歌手和黑袍牧师
在夏夜的豌豆丛中
耳语，小声呢哝

"这些，"一个人凝神倾听
"——宁静的泉水多么温柔地填平了
　　我那悲惨命运的深坑——"

Man of Few Possessions

A katydid and cricket
singer dressed in green and a priest in black robes
among peas on a summer night
whispering, at the ear

"This," a man listens attentively
"— quiet spring water so gently filled
    the deep pit of my tragic fate —"

我是别的事物

我是我的花朵的果实。
我是我的春夏后的霜雪。
我是衰老的妇人和她昔日青春
　　全部的美丽。

我是别的事物

我是我曾读过的书
靠过的墙壁　笔和梳子。
是母亲的乳房和婴儿的小嘴
是一场风暴后腐烂的树叶
——黑色的泥土

I Am Other Things

I am the fruit of my flowers.
I am the frost and snow after my spring and summer.
I am the aging woman and her past youth
      in all its beauty.

I am other things

I am the book I once read
the wall I leaned on   pen and comb
am a mother's breast and a baby's mouth
am a leaf rotting after a storm
— the black mud

壁虎

它并不相信谁。
也不比别的事物更坏。

当危险来临
它断掉身体的一部分。

它惊奇于没有疼痛的
遗忘——人类那又一次
新长出的尾巴。

Lizard

It believes no one.
No worse than other things.

When danger comes
it cuts off a part of its body.

It's amazed by the painless
forgotten — a new tail mankind
regrows.

一穗谷

每种事物里都有一眼深井。

一穗谷，你的井竖在半空中。

它幽暗，使四周的光
　　围拢。（那里，一个宇宙
鱼群在水底穿梭　而鸟儿
　　落在枝头）

你的叶柄下有一口泉水
在星辰和星辰间走动。

而你包裹漫漫长夜的果实
　　在光辉中成熟。

——我朝下倾听，一穗谷
泥土深处整座森林
　　风声的轰鸣——

An Ear of Grain

Each thing has a well.

An ear of grain, your well stands in mid-sky.

It is dim, rounding up light
        from everywhere.   (There, a universe
shoals of fish shuttle underwater   birds
        land on branch tips)

A spring of water beneath your leafstalk
ambulating between stars and stars.

Your fruits wrapped with the long night
        ripen in radiance.

— I bow and listen, an ear of grain
deep in the mud the whole forest
        the thundering of wind —

会不会有一棵树

会不会有一棵树
一棵去年的青杨
望着今年的青杨
望着今年夏天的阳光
会不会有一本书
摊开在膝盖上
插图里悄悄长出弯弯的尖须

当夜停歇在睡眠者的眼睑上
记忆和梦中出现的——
　　　　风中的芦苇　　红桑椹
炊烟和野鸟蛋
正冒犯世界的体面
它们跨越人的边缘
把时光背后的景象
一一呈现

进入此刻的仍有
比眼睛更多的眼睛
比山峦更多的山峦
一棵树躯干上的伤痕
一张书页里残存火星的征兆
一个人推着童年的铁环
　　　跑过这个夜晚

Will There Be a Tree

Will there be a tree
a Cathay poplar from last year
looking at a Cathay poplar from this year
looking at sunlight from this summer
Will there be a book
opened on both knees
sharp vines growing quietly from its illustrations

When night rests on a sleeper's eyelids
appearing in memory and dream —
                reeds in the wind   raspberries
chimney smoke and wild bird eggs
are violating the world's dignity
transcending the fringe of mankind
presenting the scenes behind time
one by one

What enters this instant includes
eyes more than eyes
mountain chains more than mountain chains
a scar on a tree trunk
omens from sparks remaining on a page
a man rolling an iron hoop from his childhood
                running through this night

现实

没有白天，没有黑夜。
没有善。也没有恶。
一群人在受苦。
仅此而已。

没有绝对的词。
这些风吹散的薄纸的灰烬。

一群人在受苦。
就是这些。

永不休耕的土地里
只有一个女人挎着光辉的篮子
默默播撒种籽。

Reality

No day, no night.
No goodness. And no evil.
A group of men suffering.
That's all.

No absolute word.
Thin paper ashes dispersed by wind.

A group of men suffering.
Just like this.

In the land that never lies fallow
only a woman with a radiant basket
silently sows seeds.

有所思

观念在反对艺术，一根木头
在反对一棵树。在这里
娱乐和晚会反对呻吟
一道篱笆阻挡着整座森林。

艺术在园子里漫步，并非意味着
园子就是艺术。何其相似
所有面孔在暴政下就是一张面孔
这一切取决于权利和黄金
市场的比率

为此可以再多一些小便盆
印刷的梵高比麦田更真实
他们无需因为没认出一条微小的裂缝而羞愧
他们，他们。
波德莱尔为何要把穷人打昏
——包括你？

交易期待着观念整齐的流水线
带着无知，或许更可怕的阴谋。
因为在这里
没有谁理会无名的流浪汉

被虎口钳紧紧夹住的一根手指的叫喊。

Meditations

Concept against art, a log
against a tree. Here
entertainment and parties against a moan and groan
A fence blocks the whole forest.

Art strolling in a garden does not mean
the garden is art. How similar
under tyranny, all faces are the same face
All of these are up to rights and gold
market ratios

To this end, add some chamber pots
Van Gogh reproductions are more original than wheat fields
They see no need for shame over missing a tiny crack
They, them.
Why did Baudelaire knock down the poor
— and you?

Trade awaits concepts in a neat pipeline
with ignorance, or a more hideous scheme.
For here
no one notices a nameless tramp

screams from a finger trapped tightly in the jaws of pliers.

现在，不可触及

——对帕斯说

米斯夸克，墨西哥小镇
你在纸页上的曙光里将它建起
在语言和真实的岩石上
在刀刃上和孤独者的眼里

而依旧是我的现在
不可触及。半空中的房间
禁锢低头下望的目光。大街拥挤的汽车
拖着钢铁欲望的外壳
立交桥无尽的缠绕，报纸新闻
更远——不可触及

我的手敲打键盘
那里不生长一棵草，也没有
最小的微风，宛如无人的古井
涟漪不超出七寸荧屏

面对一碗米饭羞愧，面对不可触及的
腐烂肠子中钻出的蒿草啜泣
瓦砾下汹涌着比海更狂暴的怒浪
足以摧毁压在额头的巨石

我的鼠标在黑暗地洞里奔窜，寻找一个
光明的出口。荒凉的楼群不可触及
语言犁头找不到泥土里
最细的草根，那门缝夹疼的一丝光亮

Now, Untouchable

— Speaking to Octavio Paz

Mixcoac, a small Mexican town
You built it up at daybreak on each page
on rocks of language and truth
on a knife's edge and in a loner's eyes

And my present remains
untouchable. The room in mid-sky
imprisons a bowed head's downward gaze. Cars in crowded streets
haul steel shells of desire
endlessly twining flyovers, journal news
further — untouchable

My hands strike at the keyboard
where not a strand of grass grows, not even
the tiniest breeze, like an abandoned old well
ripples do not surpass the seven-inch screen

Shamefully facing a bowl of rice, facing the untouchable
rotten intestines squeeze out wormwood and sobbing
Torrential waves fiercer than the sea are surging under the rubble
enough to destroy a huge rock pressing on my forehead

My computer mouse scurries in a black burrow, in search of a
bright exit. Desolate buildings are untouchable
A ploughshare of language can't find the finest grass root
in the soil, a ray of light painfully jammed in a door crack

现在，对于渴望，市场
有着满足幸福的允诺
但一个濒死者的喉咙，不可触及
羞愧在燃烧我虚弱的头顶
一场蔓延的灾难，不可触及的瘟疫
于你，是故乡，被毁坏的白蜡树
于我，是现在，也是过去
不可触及
是时间的丛林、山峦、平原、河流的痛哭……

Now, for desires, the market
holds promises that satisfy bliss
but a dying man's throat, untouchable
Shame is burning the top of my frail head
A sprawling disaster, the untouchable plague
For you, home, ruined Chinese ash trees
For me, now, also the past
Untouchable
wails of jungles, mountains, plains, and rivers of time . . .

几粒沙子

一

人们不会询问泪水。他们倾向于带来
平面的事物。在那上面有着被黑布覆盖着的
鹅卵石面包。

不幸不属于大众。那最个人的
仍然是一个吻在离开它热爱的花朵时
滴下血,增添了世界的鲜艳。

二

报纸:人质。武器。死伤人数。
每个民族占据一块版面。

炸弹的碎片中有一只活鸟
在和平国度黎明的窗外击中一个诗人的昏迷

阳光照临时的霎那撞到它眼睛里的黑。

三

有时候我忽然不懂我的馒头
我的米和书架上的灰尘。

我跪下。我的自大弯曲。

A Few Grains of Sand

1

People do not ask tears. They prefer
objects that flatten everything. With pebble bread on top
draped in black cloth.

Misfortune does not belong to the masses. Most personalized
is still a kiss leaving its adored flower
dripping blood, enhancing the world's radiance.

2

Newspapers: hostages. Weapons. Death tolls.
Each nationality occupies a page.

A bird alive in shrapnel
strikes a poet's stupor outside the dawn window of a peaceful nation

The instant sunlight arrives it hits the blackness in its eyes.

3

Sometimes I just can't understand my steamed bun
my rice and the dust on these bookshelves.

I kneel. My ego bends.

四

树叶飘落。豆子被收割。
泥土在拖拉机的犁头后面醒来。

它们放出河流和风在新的旷野上。

五

我们自身的脚镣成就我们的自由
借助痛楚那时间的铁锤。

六

所有掷向他人的石块都落到我们自己的头顶。

干渴的人，我的杯子是你的
你更早地给了我有源头的水。

七

幸福的筛子不漏下一颗微尘。
不漏下叹息、星光、厨房的炊烟
也不漏下邻居的争吵、废纸、无用的茫然。

除了一个又一个
清晨。黄昏。

八

哦，命运，我在你给我的绞索上抓住了多少
可免于一死的珍宝！

4

Leaves fall. Beans are harvested.
The soil wakes behind the tractor's ploughshare.

They release rivers and wind in the new wilderness.

5

Our own shackles create our freedom
by means of anguish the hammer of time.

6

All stones thrown at others fall on our own heads.

Thirsty one, my cup is yours
Previously you've given me water from a source.

7

A happy sieve doesn't leave behind the slightest dust.
Does not leave behind sighs, starlight, kitchen chimney smoke
nor the quarrels of neighbors, wastepaper, a useless void.

Other than one yet another
dawn. Dusk.

8

O destiny, on the rope you've given me, I seize many treasures
that could be spared from death!

变化

光线改变了物体
犹如你改变了我
此刻，出现了阴影、曲线
而从前我并不知道

这些我的影子！　我
　　运动的面孔
流星、草叶和石上的青苔
众多亲眷　　系在
我身上的细线——
你的爱与它们相等
你明了这些——
我　　世界的幸福与不幸
一颗砝码　　与一架天平

Change

Light rays change matter
the way you change me
At this instant, shadows and curves emerge
yet I didn't know

these are my shadows! My
        face in a workout
falling stars, leaves and moss on the rocks
numerous kin   fastened onto
fine lines on my body —
your love equates them
you know these —
I   the world's happiness and misfortune
a weight   and a balance

一般定律

紧张在清晨的一个懒腰中。
在拖鞋、吃饭和聊天的
粉红战壕里。

其余的是疯狂。

你所知道最紧张的
已经松弛了。

Standard Law

Tension in a morning stretch.
In pink trenches
of slippers, eating and chatting.

The rest is madness.

The greatest stress you know
has loosened.

III   CANYON IN THE BODY

木匠在刨花里……

木匠在刨花里砍出他的脸而
铁匠在镰刀和麦秆间弯腰藏着。

白发老妇在破旧的织机上
织出窈窕的腰身和花朵的大红。

在乡间，一株白杨就是
一股升起的炊烟，为了让
晚归的羊群远远看见。

我写着单纯的诗句，沿着
笔直的田畦，一溜刚播下的麦种
领着我浑身碧绿地闪出
　　　感觉的无线电。

Carpenter in the Thick of Wood Shavings . . .

The carpenter carves out his face in the thick of wood shavings while
the blacksmith stoops and hides among sickles and wheat stalks.

On a worn-out loom the old white-haired woman
weaves slender waistlines and scarlet.

In the country, a poplar is
a pillar of rising chimney smoke, for
sheep to see from afar, late on their way home.

I write simple verse, along
straight plots of land, a row of new wheat
guides my whole body, flashing in green
          radio waves of feeling.

歇晌

午间。村庄慢慢沉入
　　明亮的深夜。

穿堂风掠过歇晌汉子的脊梁
躺在炕席上的母亲奶着孩子
芬芳的身体与大地平行。

知了叫着。驴子在槽头
甩动尾巴驱赶蚊蝇。

丝瓜架下，一群雏鸡卧在阴影里
间或骨碌着金色的眼珠。

这一切细小的响动——
——世界深沉的寂静。

Siesta

Noon. The village slumps into
        a bright late night.

A draft brushes the spine of a napping man
a mother lies on a *kang* mat nursing her child
her fragrant body aligning with the earth.

Cicadas drone. At the trough a donkey
flicks its tail at mosquitoes.

Under a gourd trellis, a brood of chicks idles in the shade
golden eyes rolling from time to time.

These delicate sounds of movement —
— profound silence in the world.

只有……

只有夜晚属于梦想。
只有寂静的青杨林
槽头反刍的牲口
只有正午蜜蜂嗡嗡的飞舞——

泉水的倾听。火中的凝眸。
只有一个人轻轻脚步的风暴。
粗糙的树干将别离掩入
　　怀中——

只有风鼓起窗幔……
只有稿纸静静的水底
沉睡着万物连绵的群山——

Only . . .

Only night belongs to dreams.
Only quiet poplars
beasts of burden chewing at a trough
Only the humming waltz of bees at high noon —

Spring water listens. Fixed eyes of fire.
Only the storm of one's light footsteps.
Coarse tree bark will hide separation
                in its bosom —

Only curtains drummed by the wind . . .
Only hushed waters beneath writing paper
where endless mountains of the universe sleep —

黄昏

黄昏，我听到它秘密的窸窣。
——这里曾发生过什么？

一片年轻的楸树林走向夜晚
风拖长影子在枝干间滑过。
在它幽暗的深处
传来一棵雁肠草年迈的
　　　叹息。

我轻轻停步——倾听
　　　脚下的大地沉默无声。

Dusk

Dusk, I hear its rustling in secret.
— What happened here?

Young Manchurian catalpas walk toward night
Wind stretches shadows and slides through branches.
From its dim depth
a strand of water chickweed's aging
         sigh.

I stop gently — listening
         to the silent earth beneath my feet.

虚无

虚无，最大的在之歌

从它而来的万物在欢唱——
冉冉升起的朝阳多么辉煌！

孩子们伸手就会摸到苹果
圆满彤红地挂在碧绿的树上。

还有爱情——嘴唇渴望着嘴唇
灰烬中闪着一点发烫的火光。

白发苍苍的老人度过童年
在积木搭成的乐园旁。

是的，一切都将归于虚无
而在之美梦与它一样久长。

Nothingness

Nothingness, the greatest ode to existence

The universe it creates sings in joy —
how magnificent the slow-rising sun!

Children stretch their hands to touch apples
fully round and red on lush green trees.

And love — lips yearn for lips
a tiny scalding flame glows in ashes.

Old men with white hair spend their childhood
next to a paradise built in toy blocks.

Yes, everything will return to nothingness
the fond dream of existence just as eternal.

母亲

一个和无数个。
但在偶然的奇迹中变成我。

婴儿吮吸着乳汁。
我的唇尝过花楸树金黄的蜂蜜
伏牛山流淌的清泉。
很久以前

我躺在麦垛的怀中
爱情——从永生的荞菜花到
　　一盏萤火虫的灯。

而女儿开始蹒跚学步
试着弯腰捡起大地第一封
落叶的情书。

一个和无数个。
——请继续弹奏——

Mother

One and uncountable.
But by chance and miracle I become a mother and miracle.

The baby is suckling breast milk.
My lips have tasted rowans' golden honey
clear spring water on Mount Funiu.
Long ago

I lay in the bosom of a haystack
Love — from immortal shepherd's-purses to
          a firefly lamp.

My daughters start to toddle
trying to bend and pick up fallen leaves
the earth's first love letter.

One and countless.
— Please continue the concert —

立秋

午后。四周变暗。
仿佛剧院里沉沉大幕前的灯光。
墙角溜来突然的一阵风
把行人吹进秋天的街头。

云彩拖着阴影
掠过推铁环少年的头顶。

……再见，空荡荡的田野
　　耕完地的赶牛人。
永别了！青春——
灌木丛还在继续着你燃烧的眼神。
从你唇边流淌出蜜一样的歌声
在混浊的河水中渐渐平静。

秋天那灰蒙蒙的远方仿佛
　　寺庙的屋顶
在低垂的柳树间我瞥见
一个颤抖在往事中的幽灵。

The Start of Autumn

Afternoon. Darkens all around.
Like lights before heavy grand drapes in a theatre.
A sudden gust of wind from a corner
blows pedestrians into the autumn street.

Clouds drag shadows
over a youth's head as he rolls a hoop.

. . . Goodbye, empty field
      herder done plowing.
Farewell! Youth —
shrubs carry on your burning gaze.
Songs flow like honey off your lips
cooling off in the muddy river.

Autumn far and overcast like
            a temple's roof
Through the drooping willows I glimpse
a spirit shivering in the past.

遗失

一个人遗失在信中。书中。
遗失在手离开后的灰尘里
以及椅子　灯光后
被用过的感情的轭具
以及列车呼啸而过的阴影——

他有着树叶和云彩的形状
在他的脚印里
有着积水映出的四季的形状

有时，某人会带着他　在
沉重发炎的膝关节里——
走向郊外　旧铁轨旁
在一丛被压倒的野蒿上
与另一个他相遇——

一个人遗失在被他遗失的
　　一切事物中。

Lost

A man is lost in letters. In books.
Lost in the dust left by a hand
and a chair   behind a lit lamp
a used yoke of feelings
and the shadow of a train whizzing past —

He has the shape of leaves and clouds
In his footprint
the shape of seasons reflected in a puddle

Sometimes, someone will walk   in
a badly inflamed knee joint —
to the suburbs   near an old rail
above the overwhelmed daisy fleabanes
to meet another him —

A man is lost in everything
        he's lost.

风

风从他身体里吹走一些东西。

木桥。雀舌草叶上露珠矿灯的夜晚
一只手臂　脸　以及眼眶中
蒲公英花蕊的森林。
吹走他身体里的峡谷。
一座空房子。和多年留在
墙壁上沉默的声音。

风吹走他的内脏　亲人的地平线。
风把他一点点掏空。
他变成沙粒　一堆粉末
　风使他永远活下去——

Wind

Wind blows things away from his body.

Wooden bridge. A night of miners' lamps, dew on leaves like
                                        sparrow tongues
an arm   a face   a forest
of dandelion pistils in the eyes.
Blows away the canyon in his body.
An empty house. Silent voices
left on the wall for years.

Wind blows away his organs   the horizon of kinship.
Wind empties him little by little.
He becomes sand grains   powder
    Wind lets him live forever —

关于风景

一列飞驰的山峰。一片奔跑起来的
槐树林。田野。田野
这一片风景被词语抬起
上升。而"水果"
高悬在半空中。

那不是真的。一个奇异的梦
在河流和草丛上飞翔
被我的墨水染绿——这
模糊的语言的唇齿却接触到
给予了我全部生活的大地上

一粒红浆果的滋味。

Concerning Scenery

A line of summits speeding past. A forest of running
pagoda trees. Field. Field
Lifted by words this scenery
rises. And "fruit"
hangs in midair.

That isn't true. A strange dream
soars above rivers and grass
dyed green by my ink — yet this
vague language can touch with its lips and teeth
from the earth that gives me all this life

the taste of a red currant.

萤火虫

我的眼睛保住了多少
　　萤火虫小小的光芒！
那些秋天的夜晚
萤火虫保住了多少
　　星空、天籁、稻田的芳香！

清凉的风吹进树阴
轻轻围抱起活过的恋人
山楂树低垂的果实下
　　那互相靠近的肩膀

绿荧荧的小虫游丝一样织进
　　山林、村落、溪水的流淌
爱啊，温柔的亲娘
保住了多少往事和叹息：
众多细小的生命
保住了我幸福而忧伤的一生……

Firefly

My eyes preserve many
       tiny sparkling fireflies!
On those autumn nights
fireflies preserve many
       starry skies, sounds of nature, and rice field scents!

Cool wind blows into the shade
gently embracing lovers from this space-time
Under the drooping hawthorn fruits
       their shoulders lean close

Like spider silk green glowing bugs weave their way into
       mountain forests, hamlets, running creeks
O love, tender mother
you preserve many memories and sighs:
many tiny lives
preserve my blessed and grieving life . . .

大河村遗址

又一个大河村。
乌鸦在高高的杨树上静卧着
成群的麻雀飞过晒谷场
翅膀沾满金黄的麦芒
它们认出我。

微风还在几年前吹过
没有岁月之隔
我难道是另一个？

黄昏，长长的树影投向沙丘
又到了燃生炊火的时候
熟识的村民扛着铁锹
走在田埂上
牛驮着大捆的青草
像从前一样。我闪到一旁——

没有岁月之隔
只有大河村，这一动不动的
滔滔长河。

Ruins of the Great River Village

Another Great River Village.
Crows rest quietly on tall poplars
Sparrows fly over the grain-drying ground
wings tinted with golden wheat shine
They recognize me.

Years ago the breeze still blew
No barrier of time
Am I someone else?

At dusk, trees cast long shadows onto dunes
Time again to build a cook fire
A villager I know carries a shovel
walking the ridge
An ox carries bales of grass
as before. I dodge —

no barrier of time
only the Great River Village, this static
torrential flow of water.

令人心颤的一阵风

令人心颤的一阵风
令人心颤的另一阵风
从村庄掠过。
为什么只有树叶和麻雀
　　　只有我被风吹动?
像一束光
照亮了屋顶和瓦松
照亮了我?

据说每个人都有心灵
但是，风呵
有谁听见并复述出
你敞开秘密的恩赐的布道?

A Shuddering Gust of Wind

A shuddering gust of wind
Another shuddering gust of wind
sweeps from the village.
Why are there only leaves and sparrows
        only me moved by the wind?
Like a beam of light
illuminating the roof and its orostachys
illuminating me?

They say everyone has a spirit
but wind,
who listens and retells
your sermon, a gift that opens secrets?

在我的村庄

在我的村庄，日子过得很快
一群鸟刚飞走
另一群又飞来
风告诉头巾：
夏天就要来了。

夏天就要来了。晌午
两只鹌鹑追逐着
钻入草棵
看麦娘草在田头
守望五月孕穗的小麦
如果有谁停下来看看这些
那就是对我的疼爱

在我的村庄
烛光会为夜歌留着窗户
你可以去
因那昏暗里蔷薇的香气
因那河水
在月光下一整夜
淙潺不息

In My Village

In my village, days speed by
A flock of birds just flew away
Another flock comes
Wind tells the scarf:
Summer is coming.

Summer is coming. At noon
two quail chase each other
into the grass
Shortawn foxtails on the field's edge
watch over the sprouting May wheat
If someone stops to see these
that's his way of loving me

In my village
candlelight leaves a window open for evening song
You can go there
because its dusky rose fragrance
because the river
run endlessly
all night long in moonlight

在小店

去年的村庄。去年的小店
槐花落得晚了。
林子深处，灰斑鸠叫着
断断续续的忧伤
一个肉体的忧伤，在去年
泛着白花花悲哀的盐碱地上
在小店。

一个肉体的忧伤
在树荫下，阳光亮晃晃地
照到今年。槐花在沙里醒来
它爬树，带着穷孩子的小嘴
牛铃铛　季节的回声
灰斑鸠又叫了——

心疼的地方。在小店
离开的地方。在去年

In Xiaodian

Last year's village. Last year's Xiandian
Pagoda flowers fall too late.
Deep in the woods, a collared dove cries
sporadic sorrow
a body's sorrow, last year
on alkaline soil suffused with white grief
in Xiaodian.

A body's sorrow
under the shade of a tree, sunlight dazzles
until this year. A pagoda flower awakes in sand
It climbs a tree, with a poor child's mouth
a cowbell   the echoes of seasons
the collared dove cries again —

A place that hurts. In Xiaodian
A place left behind. Last year

其他……

我选中了一条孤零零的
消失在玉米地深处的小路。
我选中一座隐藏在槐林和
    野豌豆丛里的房屋，那里
一弯无声的渠水安静穿过。
树影　幽幽飘落的叶子
在水面上轻轻荡了一下
又沉入长长的睡乡。

我疑惑，它们都是什么？
一条路？一座房屋？还是
映照过奥菲丽雅脸庞的波光？

我要求全部。全部的。
这飘着轻尘的小径　久无人拜访的
看林人长满绿苔的房屋的墙角
以及死一样寂寞的渠水——全部的。
如此清晰　无边无际。

现在我坐下来：面对
    疯狂繁殖的景色——
——金黄的飞蝶　几片槐叶
在纸上的乐园中修筑
    它们最后的安眠——

Et cetera . . .

I choose a solitary path
vanishing into the deep cornfield.
I choose a house hidden among pagoda trees
          and vetches, where
canal water weaves quietly through a bend.
Tree shadows   soft falling leaves
a gentle stir on its surface
then deep into a long sleep.

I wonder, what are these?
A road? A house? Or
ripples of light upon Ophelia's face?

I ask for everything. Everything.
This little path in a dusty mist   an unvisited
keeper's house with corners overrun by moss
canal water lonely like death — everything.
So clear   and vast.

Now I sit down: facing
          a madly spawning scenery —
— golden butterflies   some pagoda leaves
building their last slumber
          in an Eden on paper —

旅行

旅途，穿行在万里雨中
为什么你的目光望着窗外
你的手贴在女人额头
连绵的群山　一个接一个的
隧洞　深夜里黝黑的丛林
湿淋淋草叶的沉重

你的手和目光
抚摸的是同一事物？
在它们之间你痛楚的幸福
那短暂、消逝、留在原地的
　　　一列快车——
那温柔弯曲的女人的膝盖
　　　在呼喊——
向前奔走。永不离开。

Travel

Voyage, through thousands of miles of rain
Why is your gaze looking out the window
your hand on a woman's forehead
ranges of mountains unbroken   tunnels one after
another   dark woods late at night
the weight of grass and leaves dripping wet

Do your hand and gaze
stroke the same thing?
Between them your anguished bliss
that brief, vanishing express train
        that holds right there —
a woman's tender curved knees
        are shouting —
Race on. Never leave.

野葵花

野葵花到了秋天就要被
砍下头颅。
打她身边走过的人会突然
回来。天色已近黄昏，
她的脸，随夕阳化为
金色的烟尘，
连同整个无边无际的夏天。

穿越谁？穿越荞麦花的天边？
为忧伤所掩盖的旧事，我
替谁又死了一次？

不真实的野葵花。不真实的
歌声。
扎疼我胸膛的秋风的毒刺。

Wild Sunflower

Come autumn the wild sunflower head
will be chopped off.
Those who walk past her will suddenly
turn back. Dusk soon,
with sunset, her face transforms
into golden smoke,
along the vast summer.

Through whom? A horizon of buckwheat flowers?
Old past veiled in sorrow, for whom
have I died once more?

Untrue wild sunflower. Untrue
singing.
A lethal thorn of autumn wind pricks my chest.

歌手

要赶路的夜行马车你拐弯吧
拉上最重的一捆黄谷你走吧
一生的时间对于我
还不够。　倒映在水面的星星
不是星星。曾活过的人
都已化为尘土。
我的祈祷——还不够

但我有过悠闲的时刻。在十月
看见几只麻雀掠过屋顶
撩起扑噜噜的响声
我能长出丰美的翅膀
　　　追上她们飞
我能开花，金黄或者鲜红
一直到第一场大雪降临
我看到了谁　谁就是我的：
水晶、一头花奶牛、红色的柿树
突然奔跑起来的一列山峰

会哭的事物才会活下去
我　或者任何一阵夜雨
呜咽的林涛、水声
升起到一个故乡　又
沉入光中
像绵绵不绝的山谷里的回音
再没什么可以丢失　再没什么
　　　可以被夺走

Singer

Hasty night carriage, make a turn
with the heaviest bale of wheat
A lifetime to me
isn't enough.   Stars reflected in water
aren't stars. Those who once lived
are now dust.
My prayer — isn't enough

but I'd known leisurely moments. In October
I saw sparrows skim over the roof
with gurgling sounds
I can grow lush wings
          and chase them
I can flower, golden or scarlet
until the first heavy snow
Whoever I see   becomes mine:
crystal, dairy cow, red persimmon tree
a row of summits running all at once

Things that can cry will survive
I   or a band of night rain
wind in the woods and water sobbing
rise to a hometown   then
sink into light
like undying echoes in a valley
nothing else can be lost   nothing else
          can be taken away

IV   A TREE IN MY CHEST

风中的栗树

让我活着遇到你
这足够了。

风中的栗树
我那寒冷北方的栗树
被银色的月光照亮过。
我多么想说出我所知道的
村庄的名字、打谷场
睡杜鹃和只活一个夏天的甲虫
我知道我会哭它们
一年又一年地脱离它们
在林中空地我踩着一个边
梦见它们。
忘了这些，我就会蓦然
　　熄灭。

我多么想对人说一说栗树的孤单
多想让人知道
我要你把我活着带出
　　时间的深渊

Chestnut Tree in the Wind

To meet you while alive
is enough for me.

A chestnut tree in the wind
My chestnut tree from the cold north
kindled by silver moonlight.
How I wish I could say all that I know
the village's name, the winnowing barn
sleeping cuckoos and ladybugs that only lived one summer
I know I'd cry for them
drifting away from them year after year
On some empty land in the woods I step on its edge
and dream of them.
If I forget these, I'd die out
      suddenly.

How I wish I could share with others the solitude of a chestnut tree
letting them know
I want you to bring me out alive
      from the abyss of time

柿树

下午。郑州商业区喧闹的大道。
汽车。人流。排长队人们的争吵。
警察和小贩们争着什么。
电影院的栏杆旁
——亲爱的，这儿有棵柿树
有五颗微红的果实。
灰色的天空和人群头顶
五颗红柿子在树枝上——
亲爱的，它是
这座城市的人性。

Persimmon Tree

Afternoon. A bustling boulevard in Zhengzhou's business district.
Cars. A stream of people. Brawls in a long queue.
Policemen and vendors are arguing.
By the railing of a cinema
— dear, here is a persimmon tree
with five red fruits.
Gray sky, above a sea of heads
five red persimmons on a tree branch —
dear, it is
this city's humanity.

一瞥

仿佛乡间的晨雾
远处淡紫色的
　　你肩胛上的光辉
因为太近——令人头晕的

香气弥漫：这暴露在世界暗处的
　　秘密一闪
它令人感激与此有关的
月夜、大街、菜市场的喧闹
以及所有生活中的烦恼

A Glimpse

Like morning fog in the country
distant and soft violet
      radiance on the back of your shoulder
because it is too close — enveloped in a dizzy

fragrance: exposed in dark places
      a secret dash
making one grateful for its
moonlit night, avenues, the bustle of food markets
and all of life's worries

谈论人生

他好像在讲一本什么书。
他谈论着一些人的命运。

我盯着他破旧的圆领衫出神。
我听见窗外树叶的沙沙声。

我听见他前年、去年的轻轻嗓音。
我看见窗外迅速变幻的天空。

不知何时办公室里暗下来。
他也沉默了很久很久。

四周多么宁静。
窗外传来树叶的沙沙声。

Discussing Life

He appears to be lecturing on a book.
He is discussing some people's fates.

I stare transfixed at his shabby crew neck.
I hear the rustling of leaves outside.

I hear his soft voice from years past.
I see the sky fast mutating outside.

Not knowing when the office has turned dark.
He too falls into a long, long silence.

So quiet everywhere.
The rustling of leaves outside.

危险

很可能，我是你所期望的——
一株最绿的薄荷草，非修辞的美丽
你梦中弯弯吹着的风
我是你手指的模样　　额头的明亮
你早晨的气息　　眼神
　　温和地含着忧伤

但这里埋伏着——
　　心跳停顿的空白　　呻吟
　　失望　秋天那颗粒无收的谷仓
我是你变凉的指尖　一个零
——没有余数　也没有"没有"

我不是我的宾语，一个可疑的人
我是你，亲爱的——
你的干旱　　暴雨
你的世亲与宿敌

Danger

Quite possibly, I'm what you expect —
the greenest strand of spearmint, an unrhetorical beauty
an arc of wind blowing in your dreams
I'm the look of your fingers   the shine of your forehead
your morning breath   gaze
        mildly sorrowful

But here lying in ambush —
        a pause in a heartbeat   a moan
        will disappoint   an autumn barn after a total crop failure
I'm your fingertip that turns cold   a zero
— no remainder   or a "no"

I'm not my object, someone dubious
I'm you, dear —
your drought   storm
your kin through the ages and old enemy

盲者

看，就是触摸。
手指下造物的一颗心脏的跳动
就是嘴唇从泥土中升起
然后说——

就是增殖的一片国土漫出瞳孔
又朝向它自己围拢。
就是爱向爱本身致意
比它更大
        更广阔——

这些我知道。

然而我什么都不知道——亲爱的
当我再也看不到
        一个宇宙存在于其中的
                你的眼睛

The Blind

Sight is touch.
The ticking of Nature's heart under fingers
are lips that rise from mud
then speak —

And an expanding territory overflows with pupils
then clusters around itself.
And love sends its regards to love itself
larger
    ampler —

I know these things.

Yet I don't know anything — dear
when I no longer see
        a universe within
                your eyes

惊

你睡着
做梦　奔跑
星星在天空而大海在涨潮

所有的只是一件事
你做梦　奔跑
也许这是真的
我注视着你微微颤动的睫毛

你的手告诉我我正在成为的东西：
　　　女人。
不是花
也不是匿名的诗篇
——这也是真的？
当你帮助一个女人分娩自己
我从前居然不知道
她从未出生
如此漫长地等待你今夜的口令——

Startle

You're asleep
dreaming   running
Stars in the sky as tides rise

Everything as one thing
You're dreaming   running
Perhaps it's real
I watch your eyelashes tremble

Your hand tells me what I'm becoming:
              woman.
Neither a flower
nor an anonymous poem
— is this also real?
When you help a woman deliver herself
I've no idea
she was never born
waiting so long for your password in this night —

你不在这里……

你不在这里。你将替代我的躯体
一个温暖的鸽窝
在激动又寂寞的皮肤下翻滚
你不在这首诗中。
一笔一画过于寒冷
你会答应，当我的胸腹和嘴唇轻轻恳求

你会记得她们的嗓音——
　　你可爱的名字
四周的星空曾围拢过来
俯身看到她们湿漉漉的诞生

此刻我就坐在这里　　从你的眼睛里
呈现　发育
与万物一道起伏呼吸
这是世界的而不是文字的理由：
我愿和你赤裸地睡在一起
就是这个——
我要这个——

You Are Not Here . . .

You are not here. You will replace my body
a warm dove nest
roiling beneath aroused yet lonely skin
You are not in this poem.
Each stroke each move overly cold
You will agree, when my chest and lips gently beseech

You will remember their voices —
        your lovely name
how starry skies crowded all around
bending over to see their wet birth

At this instant I sit right here   from your eyes
emerge   grow
breathe in and out with the universe
This is the reason for the world but not for writing:
I long to sleep naked with you
This —
I want this —

钉子

一

我愿意走在你的后面，以便与你同享墓冢。
那里的野草呼唤着四季，并从落叶上怜悯地收留我。

二

如此安静，聚集起整个天空的闪电。
静默的瓦松知道——我的本质屋顶上的避雷针。

三

佩戴栀子花的人过去了。人消逝，栀子花一朵朵在茶杯上燃烧。

四

生活，有多少次我被驱赶进一个句号！

五

一个中年庄稼汉的裤脚下升起了炊烟。
微风来了，最高的塔被吹成平地。

六

火石。这黑暗中不停冒烟的词。

Nails

1

I'm willing to walk behind you, so that we may share a burial mound.
Where wild grass summons four seasons, adopting me out of pity
from fallen leaves.

2

So quiet, lightning assembled from the whole sky.
Silent orostachys know — the lightning rod on the rooftop of my self.

3

Gone is the one who wore a gardenia. She disappears, gardenias burn one
by one above a teacup.

4

Life, many times have I been driven into a period!

5

Smoke rises from the bottom of a middle-aged ploughman's pants.
Here comes a breeze, the tallest pagoda is cast into flat land.

6

Flint. The word that keeps fuming in the dark.

七

寒风吹着光秃秃的树枝。
路灯把我变成幽灵。孩子的笑声沉重地盖住我的脸。
墙角旋起纸屑。
我抓住它们，紧紧地——疯狂可以是这样平静。
世界在孩子的笑声中飘浮起来。打着旋。

八

自豪于自由的枷锁可以如此坚定地对我的自由进行囚禁。
在那广袤原野里放生了自由本身的无限。

九

还能走到哪里？
我的字一步一步拖着我的床和我的碗。

十

打开这本书，它的高速公路试管里淌出的墨渍。
挖掘机履带的印刷体，土地在它日益扩大的噪叫前后退。

在它辉煌的笔杆下我们挖出我们的眼，铲断我们的手
当昨天消失。

十一

卑贱者不被允许进入文字。
刽子手来了，挥舞着笔在你们的沉默前哆嗦。

噩梦跟着他。

7

A cold wind blows on bare branches.
Streetlights turn me into a ghost. Children's laughter drapes my face.
Scraps of paper whirl in a corner.
I grab them, tightly — madness can be this calm.
The world floats in the midst of children's laughter. Whirling.

8

Chains that boast of freedom can hold my freedom in such firm captivity.
Setting free the infinity of freedom in vast fields.

9

Where else can I go?
My words are hauling my bed and my bowl step by step.

10

Open this book, ink stains are dripping out of its freeway test tube.
Fonts from an excavator's tank tread, the soil recedes before its expanding growls.

Under its splendid pen we dig out our eyes, raze our hands
as yesterday disappears.

11

Scum are not allowed in words.
Here comes the executioner, brandishing his pen and trembling at your silence.

Nightmares stalk him.

十二

愿你活着。永远活着。

——一个人对仇敌的祝福。

十三

有时，一声遥远的哭泣，一个孤单离去的背影抛出绳索
从深渊救出我。

我认出那张我曾无情击打过的脸。

十四

深夜，一列细小的花朵窸窸窣窣在爬树，沿着青色的枝条——
当人们进入悲惨的梦寐。

十五

我的忠贞的根深扎在背叛你的泥土中。
多么冷酷啊！

你知道，我爱你。

你生下我。

十六

我的毫无用处：
以它的一砖一瓦造出大海，并在它的快乐上面升起我小屋的帆。

12

May you live. Live forever.

— A blessing on one's foe.

13

Sometimes, a distant sob, a lonely departing silhouette throws a rope
to rescue me from an abyss.

I recognize the face I once struck mercilessly.

14

Late night, a row of delicate flowers climbs a tree, swishing along green branches —
as people enter their tragic dreams.

15

My loyal roots are entrenched in mud that betrays you.
How ruthless!

You know, I love you.

You gave birth to me.

16

My utter uselessness:
with bricks and tiles it builds an ocean, raising the sail of my cottage over
        its happiness.

你的山林

你的山林。此刻我
作为遗属，它是我的。
我的——灌木丛长睫下的阴影

泉水沿着青皮椴向天空喷涌。
悲愁的红晕染上杜鹃花簇。
"你不开口，但我仍能听到它。"
我平静地说。

风把峡谷拉长。
这瞬间的激流中我来不及
　　抓住你的手
——一阵夜雨骤然落下
马尾松颤抖着呜咽的肩膀

随后无边的沉默中
你把自己的脸
　　从这一切中
　　　　悄悄移走——

Your Mountain Forest

Your mountain forest. I'm now
the surviving relation, it's mine.
Mine — shadows under shrubs' long eyelashes

Along green maples spring water spouts into the sky.
Clusters of azaleas are stained in a forlorn red.
You do not speak, but I can still hear it.
I say calmly.

Wind pulls the canyon longer.
In this torrent that came in an instant I couldn't
      grab your hand in time
— a band of night rain suddenly falls
horsetail pines tremble with sobbing shoulders

In the lingering vast silence
you shift your face
    from all these
      discreetly —

山楂树

最美的是花。粉红色。
但如果没有低垂的叶簇

它隐藏在荫凉的影子深处
一道暮色里的山谷；

如果没有树枝，浅褐的皮肤
像渴望抓紧泥土；

没有风在它少年碧绿的冲动中
被月光的磁铁吸引；

没有走到树下突然停住的人
他们燃烧在一起的嘴唇——！

Hawthorn Tree

Loveliest is the flower. Pink.
But were there no clusters of drooping leaves

hidden deep in its bosky shadow
a valley at dusk;

were there no branches, their beige skin
grabbing mud like desire;

no wind in its green impulse of youth
drawn to the magnet of moonlight;

no one walking to a halt under the tree
their lips burning together — !

寄生菌

废弃的矿山，积水的深坑。
你胸口早已熄灭的炉火。

它居然有过熊熊燃烧的时光
当我们还不懂得寒冷？

我解开衣扣，让太阳晾晒
这潮湿发霉的柴堆——

它原为一双手的烈焰准备，但现在
却可笑地生出了木耳。

Parasitic Bacteria

Abandoned mines, pits accumulated with water.
Stove fire in your chest is long out.

Could it have lived in blazing times
when we still didn't know the cold?

I unbutton my blouse, let the sun dry
the damp moldy heaps of firewood —

meant for two hands' fiery flames, it is now
growing fungi absurdly.

百合

她昏了过去。

香气托起柔软的腰
慢慢把她放倒在沉醉里。

一群迷惘的蜜蜂
将它们做梦的刺
伸进花萼温柔的弯曲中。

Lily

She fainted.

A fragrance wafted up the soft waist
slowly placed her in euphoria.

A swarm of baffled bees
dipped their dreaming stings
into the tender arc of the calyx.

玫瑰

她是礼服。离开植物学或
修辞学的戏台后
也是。

洗碗布旁过于洁白的封面。

即便没有别的鲜花，她们
仍然是女王。

每一个都是。

被卑微加冕。

Rose

She is a gown. After leaving the stage
of botany or rhetoric
she still is —

An overly white front cover next to a dishrag.

Even if there are no other flowers, they
are still empresses.

Each of them.

Crowned by humility.

沙漠中的四种植物

红柳

她跟我说着河流。地下滚滚的泉水。

而砂砾和碎石埋着她的沉默。
从那里她柔弱的头颅开出粉红色湿润的花来。

沙枣树

风修剪着灰绿的叶子。阳光把最明亮的颜色给她。
　　白昼的荣耀。

她不统治。也不羡慕。
她是她自己毋须梦想的样子。
大地痛苦挤榨出的甜涩果实。

骆驼刺

沙漠造成真理的铅灰色
为了被她最小的勇气刺破。

退回沉默中的教养。在
旷日持久的干旱和疾风中她有着
对自身不公平命运的无言顺从。

仿佛在完美的幸福中。

Four Kinds of Desert Plants

Tamarisk

She speaks to me about rivers. Spring water surging underground.

Gravel and crushed stones bury her silence.
Where moist pink flowers open upon her weak skull.

Oleaster

Wind is pruning gray-green leaves. Sunlight bestows the brightest color.
      The glory of daytime.

She does not reign. Or envy.
She is the appearance she needs not dream for.
The earth squeezes out sweet astringent fruits in pain.

Camelthorn

The desert brings about the leadenness of truth
to be pierced by her slightest courage.

Withdrawn to an upbringing in silence. In
prolonged drought and gale she
submits silently to her unjust fate.

As if in perfect bliss.

梭梭柴

抓起大地。直至
把沙砾下的海提到半空中。
她倾泻，浇灌荒凉的风景以及

旅人过于容易干枯的眼睛
——带着折断绝望的力量。

Black Saxaul

Grabbing the earth. Until
the sea under the gravel is lifted into midair.
Pouring in torrents, she waters the desolate landscape

and travelers' too easily withered eyes
— with strength that breaks despair.

消失

消失。
比死亡远，比拥抱近。
我接受遗产，你所奖赏的：
　　寂静。

你的赐予，我遵从。

在这横亘的安宁中我拥有
无限的时刻。广袤夜空中的群星。

金色的你的身体在闪烁，到处都是。
金色的你的嘴唇。金色的！

麦田把它逝去的韶光种植在
我命运的屋顶。

Disappear

Disappear.
Further than death, closer to a hug.
I accept the legacy, what you reward:
      stillness.

I obey your bestowal.

In this transverse peace I own
moments of infinity. Clusters of stars in a vast night sky.

Your golden body is glimmering, everywhere.
Your golden lips. Golden!

Wheat field plants its past glory
on the roof of my fate.

枕下

　　豆芽儿从枕下拱出
孩子们藏在空豆壳里
有着芝麻大的窗口

　　老人：慢慢地
一列应有尽有的火车开始
　　退着走
落叶的鸟群从地面飞回枝头
他的时间——无始无终的圆周

　　在婚床鲜花堆簇的枕下
躺着漆黑的棺木
一双冰凉的手突然伸出
抓住新人们纠缠在一起的
　　脚趾头——

Under the Pillow

Bean sprouts arch out from under the pillow
windows the size of sesames
children hide in empty pods

Old man: slowly
a train with everything starts to shift
backward
Birds among fallen leaves return to branches
His time — an infinite circumference

Under a nuptial pillow clustered with flowers
lies a pitch-dark coffin
Two icy hands suddenly stretch out
grabbing the newlyweds' entangled
toes —

新婚

嫁给群山，嫁给
赤裸的一阵风。

嫁给蔚蓝海洋的深。

戴上六月路旁的金盏花
在一床月光的棉毯中
　　　倒下——

你来。你娶一棵松树。
娶整个海岸的潮声。
你娶初夏之夜涌动的静。

抱紧我。肺叶抱紧空气。
云从高处把祭坛放到
　　　你的唇上。

Newlywed

Married to mountains, married to
a naked gust of wind.

Married to the depth of a sky-blue ocean.

Wearing June roadside marigolds
in a cotton rug bedful of moonlight
      falling —

You come. You marry a pine tree.
Marry the tidal voice of the whole seashore.
You marry the surging silence of early summer night.

Hold me tight. Lung lobes hold air tight.
Clouds from above place an altar
      on your lips.

天山

覆过霜的白桦林变成了金子
从天山南到天山北。黑松树被风吹起波涛。
林间耕作的阳光在我胸口
　　种下一棵树。

九月的火绒草，你何时再把我点燃？
何时用你落叶的急雨
冲出我干涸心中的泉水？

星辰日夜奔走。
云在天空写一首没有句号的诗。
多年后，有人会从那棵树上跳下
背起整座天池
赶到茫茫沙漠把我救出。

Sky Mountains

White birches lined with frost turn to gold
from south to north. Wind stirs black pines into waves.
Plowing in the woods, sunlight plants
        a tree in my chest.

September Edelweiss, when will you inflame me again?
When will you wash spring water from my dried heart
with the driving rain of falling leaves?

Stars rush day and night.
Clouds write a poem with no period in the sky.
Years later, someone will jump from that tree
carrying the whole of Heaven Lake
rushing to save me from the vast desert.

还是青海湖

今天，我突然想到
那被大海遗忘在雪山和高原深处的海
那片孤零零的海
带着它的青稞、牦牛、鸥阵和鱼群
带着它的四十八条河流
仍然在距我头顶3210米的天空

奔走。奔走。奔走。

Still and All, Qinghai Lake

Today, I suddenly recall
a sea forgotten by the ocean, deep in snowy mountains and highlands
That lonely sea
brings its highland barley, yaks, gulls and fish
brings its forty-eight rivers
yet in the sky 3,210 meters above my head

Rushing. Rushing. Rushing.

V   PASSWORD IN THIS NIGHT

睡梦，睡梦……

我松开的手把你握紧
关上门以便你的穿越。

我身体里的寂静
你早已得到。

我恐惧……在彼此的凝视里
变形　缩小。

Dream, Dream . . .

My loosened hand holds you tight
The door is shut for you to pass.

You've already found
silence in my body.

I fear . . . in our gaze
to contort   and shrink.

小小的

都是那么小:
蜜蜂、玻璃珠
蜗牛的房子
母亲怀中的钮扣
都是那么小:
蚂蚁的窠、雨点
半夜谁附在耳边说的一句话

我不能分清
鸟的眼睛和花籽有什么不同
在傍晚的河边
我会把任何一个洗浴的
　　　大屁股的女人
　　　认作妈妈
我五岁,会唱很多儿歌
筐里装着红桑椹和蚂蚱

小小的幸福
小小的手
我不能做大事情
不会撒谎也不必请求原谅

Little

All so little:
bee, glass bead
snail house
button in Mother's arms
All so little:
ant nest, raindrop
a word from someone at midnight's ear

I can't tell
bird eye from flower seed
By the evening river
I'll call any bathing
      woman with big buttocks
      my mother
I'm five, can sing many songs
raspberries and grasshoppers in my basket

Little happiness
Little hands
I can't do big things
can't lie and don't need forgiveness

给佩索阿

读到你的一首诗。
一首写坏的爱情诗。
把一首诗写坏：
它那样笨拙。结结巴巴。

这似乎是一首杰作的例外标准：
敏感，羞涩。
你的爱情比词语更大。

惊惶失措的大师把一首诗写坏。一个爱着的人
忘记了修辞和语法。

这似乎是杰出诗人的另一种标准。

To Pessoa

Read one of your poems.
A badly written love poem.
To write a bad poem:
so clumsy. Stuttering.

This seems like an exceptional criterion for a masterpiece:
sensitive, shy.
Your love is greater than words.

In a panic the master has written a bad poem. A man in love
forgets rhetoric and grammar.

This seems like another criterion for great poets.

在大师的客厅里

学术里没有血渍。平静里
也没有。

深秋的菊花光着身子
在寒风里瑟瑟发抖。

从什么时候起，你不再
热爱那些聪明的著述，字典里的
伟大智慧？

你的头发越来越像枯萎的花瓣
在寒风中瑟瑟发抖！

In Maestro's Living Room

No bloodstains in academia. Nor
in silence.

Naked chrysanthemums from late fall
shiver in cold wind.

Since when do you no longer
relish those brilliant texts, great wisdom
in dictionaries?

More and more your hair looks like dried petals
shivering in cold wind!

无题

我不爱外衣而爱肉体。
或者：我爱灵魂的棉布肩窝。
宁静于心脏突突的跳动。

二者我都要：光芒和火焰。
我的爱既温顺又傲慢。

但在这里：言词逃遁了，沿着
外衣和肉体。

Untitled

I don't love the coat, I love the body.
Or: I love the soul's cotton shoulder.
Stillness within a beating heart.

I want both: light and flame.
My love is gentle and proud.

But here: words flee, along
the coat and body.

现在

我写字的手　搁在地板上的脚
离阳台一步远。
我是说：现在。已是秋天。

我给你写信。我说：现在。

这现在我从没有得到。
亲爱的，从没有。

Now

My writing hand   feet resting on the floor
a step away from the balcony.
I'm saying, *Now. It's already autumn.*

I'm writing you a letter. I say, *Now.*

A *now* I never have.
Dear, never.

秘密情郎

没有地址的地方
我找你——

一行字。以波的无声传递
送至我体内的你的声音。

你有无数冰冷的身体。
火焰里的双唇。

我活着。老去。
你从未诞生——永不死亡。

Secret Lover

A place with no address
I search for you —

A line of words. Transmitting your voice
into my body in soundless waves.

You have countless icy bodies.
Lips inside flames.

I am alive. Aging.
You are never born — immortal.

小夜曲

听，那露珠般的鸟鸣
像是清晨
排箫里的小风
　　缓缓吹过
托赛里，这是你的夜？
是被幸福照亮的你青春的脸？

音符和节奏啊
但柔情——甚至
　　诗人也不用诗句
在安魂的烛光下
收拥着凋谢的花、泪滴
收拥着生活的叹息
　　和记忆的外形

仿佛是缓慢的往事：
从前的一个夜。
一个人，从前的。

Serenade

Listen, the chirping of birds clear as dew
like an early morning
breeze in a panpipe
      slowly blowing
Toselli, is this night yours?
Your youthful face kindled by bliss?

O, notes and rhythm
But tenderness — even
      poets do not use verse
in a candlelight requiem
to embrace withered flowers and tears
to embrace life's sighs
      and the shape of memory

like slow remembrances:
once upon a night.
A woman, once upon a time.

无题

没有我们　那个月夜还会存在
还会孤独地在远方
当我们死去
被月光照亮的
年轻、幸福的脸
还会微笑、低语
在它安静的天堂：

人的骨骼不能承受
任何一片落叶的重量。

Untitled

Without us   will that moonlit night still exist
lonely and faraway
When we die
will the young, blessed face
kindled by moonlight
still smile, whisper
in its quiet heaven:

A human skeleton cannot bear
the weight of any fallen leaf.

不同的一座山

透过铁条回望——
你的明眸的闪亮
光明的额角
你的手痛苦地张开又握紧
你裂成两半的影子
在告别——朝着不同的方向

每个人都清楚
这大概就是人们所说的
　　　爱情——
放肆　　勇敢
独自放射光芒

而你在深夜藏起星星
数点暗淡下去的悲愁

但在另一个地方
　　一座山不断隆起
　　　　——为了接近天堂

A Different Mountain

Looking back through iron bars —
the sparkle in your eyes
bright forehead
your hands opening and clenching in pain
your shadow split in two
bidding farewell — in different directions

Everyone knows
this is probably what they call
      love —
unbridled   brave
exuding radiance on its own

And you hide stars late at night
count the dimming sorrow

But somewhere else
      a mountain keeps swelling
          — to be closer to heaven

爱情物理学

观察：我看见天空
想到阳光也照在你的脸上
在某一条街道
我的脚印会与旧日的你重叠
我感谢每一个汉字
你不得不和我一样
用你可爱的嘴唇说出它们
还有空气——
其中有你的气息
就在呼吸之间
充满了我温暖的肺腑
——你无处不在
何曾远离？

我知道物理学的贡献
波粒二重性——现在
我如何把你确定？
既然你无处不在
就是哪里也没有你
我苦恼于我的眼睛——它是
从我体内挖去的那一部分——
等待你径直走到我面前
像世界一样把它们
堆满

The Physics of Love

Observe: I see the sky
think of sunlight also shining on your face
On a street
my footprints will overlap you from the old days
I thank each Chinese character
like me you have to say
them aloud with your lovely lips
And air —
your breath within
imbues my warm lungs
between each breathing
— you're everywhere
are you ever far?

I know the contribution of physics
wave-particle duality — now
how can I define you?
Since you're everywhere
you're nowhere to be seen
My eyes vex me — they are
the part that's dug from my body —
waiting for you to walk right up to me
like the world piling
them up

影子

在一座深秋的树林里
我和一棵紫楝树向前奔走
和整座树林　低矮的灌木丛
一条从容弯曲的水沟
我和厚厚的树叶迅速移动
拖着长长的影子——

不能想象没有阴影的事物
一座房屋有它背阴处灰色的
面孔。一张纸有薄而光滑的
脊骨。字，它的影子
　　——相反的词。
在令人放心的阴影处

有存在　那最安全的保证
是肉眼可见的世界的完整
　　——既不在全然的黑暗
也不在全然的可怖的光中——

Shadow

In late autumn woods
I race alongside a chinaberry tree
and the whole woods   short shrubs
a calm meandering gully
I move swiftly with thick leaves
dragging long shadows —

What is matter without shadow
A house has its shady gray
face. A piece of paper, its thin glossy
spine. Word, its shadow
    — the antonym.
In the reassuring shade

exists   the surest guarantee
a world's integrity seen by the naked eye
    — neither in sheer dark
nor in sheer ghastly light —

一件事情

关掉灯。
我　摸着桌子
在黑暗中

我要坦白
一件事情。交待
它的经过。

——这个世界对我的失望。
现在它
扎在我的肉体里。
就像从前
它的信任　爱
留在我的肉体里。
请允许我说
让失望吐出它的血块——

在黑暗中
谢谢黑暗的倾听
谢谢深夜　　我四周的
墙壁　桌椅和怜悯
虽然你们沉默
你们无所不知——

One Thing

Lights off.
I   touch a table
in the dark

I want to confess
one thing.   To explain
what happens.

— the world's disappointment with me.
Now it
anchors in my flesh.
Just like how
its trust   love
once lingered in my flesh.
Please let me say
let disappointment vomit blood clots —

In the dark
I thank darkness for listening
thank late night   my surrounding
walls   table, chairs and sympathy
Despite your silence
you know everything —

悲哀

不要朝我微笑吧：
我所有被称之为美德的东西都源于
　　它曾经触及过罪恶。

Grief

Don't smile at me:
everything seen as my virtues stems from
    virtue once in touch with sin.

诗人的工作

一整夜，铁匠铺里的火
呼呼燃烧着。

影子抡圆胳膊，把那人
一寸一寸砸进
铁砧的沉默。

A Poet's Work

All night long, a fire in the forge
burns and howls.

A shadow frees its arms, pounding the man
inch by inch
into the silence of the anvil.

Notes

Fiona Sze-Lorrain wishes to thank Susan Thomas, Sally Molini, Maryanne Hannan, Thomas Moran, Naomi Long, Jeffrey Greene, and Christopher Mattison.

"Vérité"

This poem was written in memory of several hundred thousand lives lost during a series of catastrophic dam collapses due to Typhoon Nina in the area of the Huai River, South Henan in August 1975. For thirty years, the death toll was classified. Located between the Yellow River and the Yangtze, the Huai region has, over the centuries, an infamous history of disastrous floods.

"Death of a Cobbler"

Modern Chinese writer and poet Xu Yunuo 徐玉诺 (1893–1958) was a native of Henan and a literary figure from the May Fourth period. Best known for his poetry collection, *Garden of the Future* (1922), his representative writings include the poem, "Ask the Cobbler" (1922) and short story, "A Broken Shoe" (1923).

"Meditations"

One of the prose poems in Baudelaire's *Le Spleen de Paris* (1869) is entitled *"Assommons les pauvres !"* ("Knock Down the Poor!")

"Siesta"

Often found in northern Chinese households, a *kang* bed is a masonry or earthern platform. It is heated in winter by a stove fire underneath, or spread with mats.

"Ruins of the Great River Village"

First discovered in the autumn of 1964, the Ruins of the Great River Village — also known as the Ruins of Dahe Village, a primitive village from the Neolithic Era — are located in the northeast suburbs of Zhengzhou, Henan. The site covers over forty million square meters with ruins and relics from the prehistorical cultures of the Central Plain: the Yangshao (5000–3000 BC), Longshan (3000–2000 BC), and Erlitou (1900–1500 BC) cultures during the New Stone Age, as well as the early Shang (1600 BC) culture.

"In Xiaodian"

Xiaodian — literally translated as "Small Shop" — is a village located in Baofeng county, Henan province.

"Sky Mountains"

Literally translated as "Sky Mountains" or the "Heavenly Mountains," Tianshan is a large mountain system of Central Asia.

Tianchi, also known as "Heaven Lake" or "the Heavenly Lake," is located in Xinjiang on the northern side of the Bogda Mountains, part of the eastern range of Tianshan.

JINTIAN SERIES OF CONTEMPORARY LITERATURE

Flash Cards
Yu Jian
Translated by Wang Ping & Ron Padgett

The Changing Room
Zhai Yongming
Translated by Andrea Lingenfelter

Doubled Shadows
Ouyang Jianghe
Translated by Austin Woerner

A Phone Call from Dalian
Han Dong
Edited by Nicky Harman
Translated by Nicky Harman, Maghiel van Crevel,
Yu Yan Chen, Naikan Tao, Tony Prince & Michael Day

Wind Says
Bai Hua
Translated by Fiona Sze-Lorrain

I Can Almost See the Clouds of Dust
Yu Xiang
Translated by Fiona Sze-Lorrain